Read and Play
Farm Machines

by Jim Pipe

Stargazer Books

Mankato, Minnesota

farm

What machines work on a **farm**?

3

plow

4

A tractor **plows**.

5

spread

6

This machine **spreads** manure.

spray

8

This plane **sprays** crops.

pick

This **picks** cotton.

This **picks** grapes.

11

harvest

These machines **harvest** corn.

13

bale

14

This makes hay **bales**.

15

dig

This machine **digs** up crops.

16

17

chop

This **chops**
up trees.

19

What do I do?

bale

plow

chop

spread

20 Match the words and pictures.

How many?

Can you count the farm machines? 21

What noise?

Buzz!

Whoosh!

Brrm! Brrm!

Crunch!

22 Can you sound like a farm machine?

Index

For Parents and Teachers

Questions you could ask:

p. 2 What farm machine can you see on this page?
A red tractor is parked in the barn on page 2.

p. 4 What is plowing? As a tractor pulls a plow, it digs long grooves in the soil called furrows that a farmer uses to plant (sow) seeds.

p. 6 Why is manure spread on the soil? Nutrients in the manure (animal dung) help the crops grow. The manure has a very strong smell!

p. 8 Can you see the clouds of spray? The plane sprays the crops with chemicals to stop weeds from growing, and to stop pests such as insects from eating the farmers' crops.

p. 10 Can you see the cotton? The fluffy white seeds are used to make the cotton in shirts and jeans.

p. 12 Can you see how the corn is harvested? The combine harvester cuts the corn and separates the yellow grain (the dried form of the corn kernels we eat) from the rest of the plant. It pours the grain into a trailer pulled by the tractor.

p. 14 Can you see the hay bale? This baler picks up the loose hay or straw on the ground and packs it into a neat bundle called a bale.

p. 16 Why do you think this machine is digging up the ground? Some crops we eat, such as potatoes, carrots, and beets, are the roots of plants so they grow under the ground.

p. 18 What is made from wood? e.g. timber houses, floors, furniture, tools, toys, paper, and cardboard.

Activities you could do:

• Ask the reader to draw a farm machine and label the different parts, e.g. cab, wheels, engine, cutters, rollers.

• Plan a day for children to bring toy tractors and other farm machines to school and encourage them to share information about these machines.

• Show pictures of different kinds of crops, e.g. corn, potatoes, fruit, cotton, hay and ask how they might be harvested, e.g. picked, cut, dug up.

© Aladdin Books Ltd 2009

Designed and produced by
Aladdin Books Ltd

First published in 2009 in the United States by
Stargazer Books,
distributed by
Black Rabbit Books
PO Box 3263
Mankato, MN 56002

Library of Congress Cataloging-in-Publication Data
Pipe, Jim, 1966
  Farm machines / Jim Pipe.
    p. cm. — (Read and play)
  Includes bibliographical references and index.
  Summary: "In very simple language and photographs, describes farm machines. Includes quizzes and games"--Provided by publisher.
    ISBN 978-1-59604-176-9 (alk. paper)
  1. Agricultural machinery--Juvenile literature. I. Title.
S675.25.P57 2009
631.3--dc22
2008015299

Series consultant
Zoe Stillwell is an experienced preschool teacher.

Photocredits:
l-left, r-right, b-bottom, t-top, c-center, m-middle
All photos from istockphoto.com except: 6-7, 14-15, 20tr & bl, 23tr & bl—courtesy New Holland. 10, 12-13, 18-19, 21—courtesy John Deere.